CROSSING THE BORDER

IMMIGRANTS OF EXTRAORDINARY ABILITY

CATHLEEN SMALL

LUCENT PRESS

Published in 2018 by
Lucent Press, an Imprint of Greenhaven Publishing, LLC
353 3rd Avenue
Suite 255
New York, NY 10010

Produced for Lucent by Calcium
Designer: Jeni Child
Picture researcher: Rachel Blount
Editors: Sarah Eason and Nancy Dickmann

Picture credits: Cover: Shutterstock: ChaNaWiT (left), Gods Kings (bottom right), Vinokurov Kirill (top), Monkey Business Images (bottom), (bottom left), Pixfly (center), Sirtravelalot (right); Inside: DVIDS: Sgt. Bobby J. Yarbrough 22; Shutterstock: Anyaivanova 18–19, Brandon Bourdages 46–47, Dennizn 50, Dragon Images 16, Dwphotos 12–13, 45br, Emka74 30, Everett Historical 4–5, Helga Esteb 14, 43, 48, Featureflash Photo Agency 59, Fstockfoto 44–45t, Jack Fordyce 35, JRP Studio 8, JStone 58, Karelnoppe 53, Glenn Kershner 57, Vinokurov Kirill 6, Lens-68 20–21, Benny Marty 56, Michaeljung 27, Monkey Business Images 17, Mr. Pics 49, Myvisuals 10, Ne3p 11, Nejron Photo 7, Photo Works 38, Lev Radin 29br, Rawpixel.com 60–61, RoidRanger 51, Santypan 15, Saraporn 55, Joe Seer 33, 39, Spotmatik Ltd 26, Syda Productions 23, Narith Thongphasuk 24, Wavebreakmedia 28–29t, Yakub88 41; Wikimedia Commons: Keith Allison 42, Bilsen, Joop van/Anefo 40, Financial Times photos 52, Eva Rinaldi 36–37, Rowland Scherman 34, U.S. Marine Corps/PFC G. Durbin 31, U.S. National Archives and Records Administration 32.

Library of Congress Cataloging-in-Publication Data

Names: Small, Cathleen.
Title: Immigrants of extraordinary ability / Cathleen Small.
Description: New York : Lucent Press, 2018. | Series: Crossing the border | Includes index.
Identifiers: ISBN 9781534562295 (library bound) | ISBN 9781534562301 (ebook) | ISBN 9781534562790 (paperback)
Subjects: LCSH: Immigrants--United States--History--Juvenile literature. | Immigrants--United States--Biography--Juvenile literature. | United States--Emigration and immigration--History--Juvenile literature.
Classification: LCC JV6450.S63 2018 | DDC 305.9'06912092273--dc23

Printed in the United States of America

CPSIA compliance information: Batch #CW18KL: For further information contact Greenhaven Publishing LLC, New York, New York at 1-844-317-7404.

Please visit our website, www.greenhavenpublishing.com. For a free color catalog of all our high-quality books, call toll free 1-844-317-7404 or fax 1-844-317-7405.

CONTENTS

CHAPTER 1

EXTRAORDINARY ABILITY AND THE O-1 VISA

North America was populated by Native American peoples for thousands of years before Europeans arrived and colonized their lands, often with force. The Pilgrims were some of the first settlers to come to North America, seeking religious freedom. They were followed by immigrants from other European nations as well. Some were seeking similar religious freedom, while others hoped for a better life or safety from persecution or tense political situations in their home countries.

Over time, European immigrants came to the United States set up farms or work in the fur trade. Europeans kidnapped and enslaved Africans, and brought them by force to work on these plantations and farms. Indentured servants came from all over Europe, working in slave-like conditions to eventually earn their freedom. The Spanish populated the west and southwest, while Mexico slowly defined its boundaries. Asian immigrants came to take part in California's Gold Rush, and later

to work on the Transcontinental Railroad. Many immigrants found work in the cities that sprang up, particularly near shipping ports.

Not Always Accepted

Immigrants settled in pockets around the developing United States, and while many citizens thought of the country as a melting pot, it was actually very segregated. Europeans brought people from Africa against their will as slaves—and even when they gained freedom, they were strictly segregated from white society and continued to experience intense discrimination. Asian immigrants were met by white Americans with suspicion and often faced discrimination too. Immigrants from European countries were welcomed, but not without suspicion. They often faced harsh conditions upon entering the United States.

Still, many people longed to come, because the United States offered freedoms they could not always find in their home countries. And it often meant a better life. That is still the case now, when people from other countries flock to the United States, both with and without documentation.

Slaves were forced to work on plantations, farms, and railroads.

Ways to Enter

The United States has generally been seen as a safe haven for people whose home countries are war-torn or devastated by natural disaster, or for those who face religious persecution. People from these countries often seek a new home in the United States. They are usually classified as either a refugee or an asylee. At the moment, there are limits and a lot of uncertainty about what refugees and asylees the United States will allow in, but in general these populations have made up a significant number of immigrants each year.

Other immigrants come over under any of the many different types of visas available. The circumstances under which immigrants can attempt to come to the United States are too many to mention. Often they involve the individual having some close family member who is already living as a citizen of the United States, but there are other reasons, too.

There are numerous types of visas for people wanting to enter the United States.

Extraordinary Ability

There is one very special category under which immigrants can come to the United States: as a person qualifying for a visa based on extraordinary ability. Visas for immigrants with extraordinary ability include the O-1 and EB-1 visas, though there are other related visas as well.

The O-1 visa, along with other visas in the O classification, was created in 1990, under the Immigration Act of 1990. Before this law, individuals with extraordinary ability were classified under H-1B visas, which were designed for temporary foreign workers in some fields. However, Congress decided that for individuals with extraordinary ability in the arts, sciences, education, business, athletics, or movie or television production, a separate visa category should exist.

The Immigration Act of 1990, which was authored by Senator Ted Kennedy and signed into law by President George H.W. Bush on November 29, 1990, also created the EB classification of visa. The EB visas are all job-based immigration visas, but the EB-1 is specifically for immigrants of extraordinary ability.

Athletes with exceptional ability may be eligible for Extraordinary Ability visas.

PROVING THEIR CASE

These visas don't mean that anyone with a talent can gain entry to the United States. Petitioners must provide evidence to prove that they have extraordinary ability. The band One Direction is based in London but has toured and performed in the United States. Proving their "extraordinary ability" likely wasn't too difficult, given that they had finished third on the British television show **The X Factor** ***and had a huge fan base on social media.***

The O-1 Visa

For those who can prove they are among the cream of the crop in their field, the extraordinary ability visas are a good way to gain entry to the United States. The O-1 visa is probably the best-known visa for people in this category. Technically, U.S. Citizenship and Immigration Services (USCIS) calls this visa the "Individuals with Extraordinary Ability or Achievement" visa.

The O-1 is considered a nonimmigrant visa, because it is only temporary. People holding an O-1 visa are not on a track to become permanent United States residents or citizens, and thus they are considered nonimmigrants. It's a funny term, since one might automatically think that a nonimmigrant is someone who is staying in their home country! In this case, the individual is traveling to another country for an extended stay—just not with the intention of it being permanent.

Musicians coming to the United States for a concert tour can apply for an O-1 visa.

Who Is Eligible?

The O-1 visa is offered to nonimmigrants who have shown extraordinary ability in the sciences, arts, education, business, or athletics. It's also offered to nonimmigrants who have shown extraordinary achievement in the movie or television industries, and who have been nationally or internationally recognized for their achievements in this field.

CLASSES OF O-1 VISA

The O-1 classification is actually broken down into several subclassifications:

- ***O-1A: for individuals who have shown extraordinary ability in the sciences, education, business, or athletics.***
- ***O-1B: for individuals who have shown extraordinary ability or achievement in the arts or in the movie or television industry.***
- ***O-2: for people who will accompany a nonimmigrant with O-1 classification specifically for the purposes of assisting with an event or performance. For a person to receive an O-2 visa, the person's contribution to the O-1 nonimmigrant's performance or event must be essential. If the person with the O-1 visa can perform their duties without the assistance of the O-2 applicant, then the O-2 visa will be denied.***
- ***O-3: for spouses and children of nonimmigrants granted O-1 or O-2 visas.***

Eligibility for the O-1 Visa

The O-1 visa is a temporary visa. To be granted an O-1 visa, the nonimmigrant must demonstrate extraordinary ability or achievement in their field. This is generally determined by the person's national or international acclaim for their achievements.

Demonstrating Ability

In the case of immigrants of extraordinary ability in the sciences, education, business, or athletics, the nonimmigrants must demonstrate a level of expertise in the subject matter that is above that of most other people in the field. In the case of immigrants of extraordinary ability in the arts or in the movie or television industry, they must have demonstrated distinction in their field—generally being regarded as renowned or leading personalities in their particular segment of the arts. Nonimmigrants in both categories must also be coming to the United States on a temporary basis, for the purpose of a performance or for continuing their work in their field.

Although some of the most famous Extraordinary Ability visa holders work in the arts, scientists may also apply.

Application Process for the O-1 Visa

Petitioners seeking an O-1 visa for a beneficiary to come to the United States must file Form I-129, Petition for Nonimmigrant Worker, no more than a year before the time they intend to be in the United States. Generally, the form should be filed at least 45 days before the nonimmigrant is scheduled to arrive. In this case, the beneficiary is the nonimmigrant, and the petitioner is the person or firm who has asked the nonimmigrant to come to the United States for work or event purposes.

This type of visa requires a written opinion from a peer group about the nonimmigrant's ability. This written opinion is known as a consultation. Generally, the peer group writing the consultation would be a labor union or other labor organization, or a management organization with expertise in the nonimmigrant's particular field. The consultation must be submitted with a watermark or other identifying mark to confirm that it is valid and not a forgery.

SPECIAL CIRCUMSTANCES

In some cases, the consultation requirement is waived. One example of this is if the nonimmigrant is seeking to reenter the United States to perform the same services as they have performed in the United States within the past two years. If this is the case, they can submit a waiver request and send a copy of the previous consultation. So, for example, if a foreign actress comes to the United States to work on a movie, and she had worked in the United States on another movie within the previous two years, she would likely not have to obtain a new consultation. These waivers can make things easier for someone like British actor Robert Pattinson, who filmed three movies in the Twilight series in the United States.

Movie crews may use Extraordinary Ability visas to enter the United States to work on a movie.

Supplying Documentation

Petitioners for nonimmigrants seeking an O-1 visa must submit a contract showing the services that the beneficiary will perform. The petitioner must also provide an itinerary of the events or activities that the beneficiary will be engaging in while in the United States. The itinerary does not need to provide exhaustive detail, but it must show that there is a good reason for the nonimmigrant to be in the United States during a particular time period. For example, the petitioner for a European band coming to the United States for a concert tour would submit an itinerary of the band's tour dates.

The documentation required for a foreign band to come to the United States on a concert tour can be quite extensive.

Evidentiary Criteria

To receive an O-1A or O-1B visa for an immigrant of extraordinary ability, the petition must provide certain evidentiary criteria for the nonimmigrant. This is to prove their claim to "extraordinary ability." For an O-1A visa, the petitioner can provide evidence that the nonimmigrant has received a major award gaining them international recognition, such as a Nobel Prize. If the nonimmigrant has not won such an award, the petitioner can provide proof of at least three of the following:

- Nationally or internationally recognized prizes or awards for excellence
- Membership in associations that require exceptional achievement, as determined by experts in the field
- Published material in major outlets that demonstrates the nonimmigrant's excellence
- Evidence of original contributions of major significance
- Authorship of scholarly articles in professional journals or other major outlets
- A significant salary in the field that would be gained by demonstrating excellence
- Participation as a judge of others' work in the field
- Employment in an essential capacity for distinguished organizations

EXTRAORDINARY ABILITY VISAS BY THE NUMBERS

The number of O-1, O-2, and O-3 visas issued each year has been steadily growing. In 1997, there were 3,345 O-1 visas issued by embassies and consulates outside of the United States, along with 1,848 O-2 visas and 748 O-3 visas. A decade later, in 2007, those numbers had more than doubled, to 7,653 O-1 visas, 4,218 O-2 visas, and 2,238 O-3 visas. And in 2015, the most recent year for which data is available, the numbers had jumped again, though not quite as significantly: 13,865 O-1 visas were issued, 5,792 O-2 visas were issued, and 4,023 O-3 visas were issued.

Criteria for the O-1B Visa

In the case of the O-1B visa, the petitioner can submit evidence that the nonimmigrant has won or been nominated for a specific prominent award in the field, such as an Oscar, Emmy, or Grammy. If this isn't the case, the petitioner can submit evidence of at least three of the following:

- Performance in a lead or starring role in productions that have a distinguished reputation
- Performance in a critical role for organizations that have a distinguished reputation
- National or international recognition for the nonimmigrant's achievements in their field
- A record of commercial or critically acclaimed success
- Significant recognition for achievements their field
- A high salary that would be indicative of the nonimmigrant's success in their field

The O-1B visa is for nonimmigrants working in the arts, including those who work in the movie or television industry. The evidentiary criteria can usually be demonstrated by critical reviews of performances, articles in major trade publications, nominations for awards, or box office receipts showing commercial success.

Grammy nominees and winners are eligible to apply for O-1B visas.

Application Process for the O-2 Visa

Support staff for people entering on an O-1 visa may be able to enter under an O-2 visa.

People entering the United States to assist an O-1 visa holder need an O-2 visa. The application process for this is very similar to the process for the O-1 visa. One difference, though, is in the evidentiary criteria. The evidentiary criteria for a nonimmigrant under an O-2 visa must show that the physical presence of the person requiring an O-2 visa is essential to the person with an O-1 visa's work in the United States.

For example, in the case of a movie being filmed in the United States, the star of the movie would require an O-1 visa to enter. However, any support staff traveling with that actor would require an O-2 visa. They would have to provide evidence that they were necessary to the production of the movie. These support staff might be hairstylists or makeup artists who had worked with the actor on the same movie in another country. There are qualified hairstylists and makeup artists already in the country who could work on the movie. However, the movie's producers could argue that if the movie is shooting in several countries, the same hairstylists and makeup artists would be needed throughout the shooting. This would ensure that the actor's look remains consistent in different scenes of the movie.

Next Steps

Once all the evidentiary criteria, consultations, and applications have been reviewed and approved, the nonimmigrant can actually apply for the visa. They must do so at a United States embassy or consulate.

Length of Stay

Under the O-1 or O-2 visas, nonimmigrants can stay in the United States for up to three years. If they require an extension, USCIS will potentially grant extensions of up to one year at a time. To request an extension, the petitioner must file another Form I-129 with USCIS and provide a copy of the nonimmigrant's Form I-94, Arrival/Departure Record, along with a statement explaining why an extension is required. If spouses or children of the nonimmigrant also wish to extend their stay, they must file with USCIS Form I-539, Application to Extend/Change Nonimmigrant Status, along with appropriate supporting documentation.

The nonimmigrant will be allowed to enter the United States up to ten days before the visa takes effect and must leave within ten days after the visa ends. However, they can only work in the United States during the visa period—not in the ten-day grace period before or after.

Holders of O-1 or O-2 visas must be mindful of their visa's expiration date, and leave the country within ten days once it expires.

MORE ABOUT THE O-1 VISA

For many types of visas, there are restrictions on the countries from which individuals can apply, as well as quotas for how many visas will be issued in a given year. This is generally not the case with O-1 visas. Normally, people from any country can apply for an O-1 visa, and there are no quotas limiting the number that USCIS will grant. However, many people have been turned down in the past, including some notable celebrities. For example, British singer Lily Allen was banned from the Unites States after her visa was revoked for assaulting a photographer in the UK. Another UK-born singer, Amy Winehouse, was denied a visa based on her history of drug convictions in other countries.

Children of O-1 and O-2 nonimmigrants can often join their parents in the United States by getting an O-3 visa.

Rights for Family Members

United States immigration policies generally favor keeping families together, so spouses and children of O-1 or O-2 nonimmigrants are often granted O-3 visas to join the nonimmigrant. However, these family members are not allowed to work in the United States under an O-3 visa. They can go to school, though, on a part-time or full-time basis.

CHAPTER 2

EMPLOYMENT-BASED IMMIGRATION

The O visas are common ones for individuals with extraordinary ability. However, there is another type of visa issued for such individuals, which is based on employment. These visas are divided into five categories, but the first two classifications are the most common ones for individuals with extraordinary ability.

The EB-1 Visa

U.S. Citizenship and Immigration Services refers to the EB-1 visa as "Employment-Based Immigration: First Preference EB-1." That's a complicated way of saying that if an individual has extraordinary ability in their field of work, if they're considered an outstanding professor or researcher, or if they're a multinational executive or manager, they may be able to obtain an EB-1 visa. Unlike the O visas, the EB-1 visa is not a temporary visa—it is designed for people seeking permanent residence in the United States.

Eligibility for the EB-1 Visa

Eligibility for the EB-1 visa is broken down into three categories: extraordinary ability, outstanding professor or researcher, or multinational manager or executive. The first two categories require specific, extensive evidence to prove that an individual meets the eligibility requirements.

Extraordinary Ability

Individuals with extraordinary ability who wish to be granted an EB-1 must be able to show that they have earned national or international acclaim for their ability in the sciences, arts, education, business, or athletics. Unlike the O-1 visa, applicants for this type of visa do not need to have an offer of employment in the United States. They only need to meet the eligibility criteria and be able to provide evidence to prove they have done so. In general, they must provide evidence to prove that they meet at least three of the following ten criteria:

- Receipt of a national or international prize or award for excellence
- Membership in associations that require their members to demonstrate exceptional achievement
- Publication of interviews or stories about the individual in major media or professional publications
- Participation as a judge of others' work in the individual's field
- Contributions of major significance in the scientific, academic, athletic, or business field
- Authorship of articles in major media publications or professional journals
- Display of artistic work at exhibitions or showcases
- Performance in a critical role in a distinguished organization
- A high salary compared to others in the field, which serves as proof of high achievement in the field
- Commercial success in the performing arts

EB visas can be an option for researchers, such as those in scientific fields.

Major Awards

An exception is made if the individual has won a major award, such as a Nobel Prize, a Pulitzer Prize, an Oscar, or an Olympic medal. In such cases, the award is enough evidence of the individual's extraordinary ability.

THIRD PREFERENCE EB-3

Another classification of Employment-Based Immigration visa is the EB-3. Skilled workers whose jobs require a minimum of two years of training or experience and are not seasonal may be eligible for this visa category. Professionals whose jobs require at least a bachelor's degree and who are working in the field in which they hold their degree may also be eligible. Finally, workers in unskilled labor fields that require less than two years of training or experience may also be eligible, as long as their jobs are not temporary or seasonal.

Foreign professors often visit U.S. universities for limited-term teaching assignments.

Outstanding Professorship or Research

Outstanding professors or researchers can be granted an EB-1 visa if they can demonstrate that they have achieved international recognition for their contributions to their particular academic field. For this category of EB-1 visa, there are a few guidelines that must be met. The individual must have at least three years of teaching or research experience in their particular academic field.

Applicants must also be coming to the United States to pursue a tenure-track teaching position or a similar research position at a U.S. university or other institution of higher learning. They must have an offer of employment from a U.S. university or research facility. The university or research facility that is offering employment to the individual must file the petition for the visa—the individual cannot file it themselves.

If they meet all of these requirements, individuals applying for this type of EB-1 visa must also provide documentation to prove that they meet at least two of the following six criteria:

- Receipt of major prizes or awards for outstanding achievement in their field
- Membership in associations that require their members to demonstrate exceptional achievement in their field
- Published material in professional publications about the individual's work in their particular field of study
- Participation as a judge of others' work in the individual's field
- Original scientific or scholarly research contributions in the individual's field
- Authorship of scholarly books or articles in the field. Articles must be published in scholarly journals with international circulation

FOURTH PREFERENCE EB-4

Another classification of Employment-Based Immigration visa is the EB-4. This category of visa is open to so-called "special immigrants." It covers a broad range of potential immigrants, including religious workers, broadcasters, members of the armed forces, employees in the Panama Canal Zone, certain types of doctors, Afghan and Iraqi translators, Afghan and Iraqi nationals who have provided faithful service in support of the United States, employees of some international organizations and their families, international employees of the United States government, and special immigrant juveniles (foreign children in the United States who have been abandoned, abused, or neglected).

The U.S. military often employs translators, such as Dinar Hasan, who translates for the Marine Corps in Afghanistan.

MANAGERS AND EXECUTIVES

Multinational managers or executives who wish to be granted an EB-1 visa must have worked for at least one year outside of the United States for a firm or corporation. They must also be seeking entry to the United States for the purpose of continuing employment with that firm or corporation, or with one of its subsidiaries or affiliates.

Executives who apply for an EB-1 visa must work for a company that has been established in the United States for at least a year.

The year that the individual has worked for the firm or corporation must have taken place within the three years preceding the request for the EB-1 visa. In other words, say that a person had worked as a manager for Roche (an international pharmaceutical firm headquartered in Switzerland) five years ago. If they then wanted to come to the United States to work as a manager for Roche at one of its U.S. offices, they would not be eligible for the EB-1 visa, because their international employment with Roche was too far in the past.

For this category of EB-1 visa, the employer must petition for the individual's visa. The employer must have been established as a business in the United States for at least one year. So, for example, a company based in Germany could not open its first U.S. office and then immediately petition to have German nationals come to the United States under EB-1 visas to work at the new office.

Who Applies?

For two of the three categories of EB-1 visa, the individual's employer must file Form I-140 (Petition for Alien Worker) with USCIS. However, individuals applying for an EB-1 visa under the extraordinary ability category can file their own Form I-140 with USCIS.

The EB-2 Visa

If a person's ability in a field is exceptional, but not necessarily extraordinary, they may be eligible to receive an EB-2 visa. The official name for this visa is "Employment-Based Immigration: Second Preference EB-2." It is designed for individuals who hold an advanced degree (master's degree or higher) or its equivalent in a particular field and are seeking to come to the United States to work in that field.

Eligibility for the EB-2 Visa

Eligibility for the EB-2 visa is broken down into three categories: advanced degree, exceptional ability, and national interest waiver. Each category requires specific, extensive evidence to prove that an individual meets the eligibility requirements.

Graduates in a particular field may be able to get an EB-2 visa if they plan to work in the field in which they hold their degree.

Advanced Degree

To be eligible for this EB-2 visa category, individuals must be applying for a U.S. job that requires an advanced degree, and they must possess that degree or equivalent experience. In this case, equivalent experience is defined as a bachelor's degree in a particular field plus five years of experience working in that field. To prove they meet these criteria, individuals must provide one of the following:

- An official academic record showing they hold the advanced degree (from a U.S. university or foreign equivalent)
- An official academic record showing they hold a bachelor's degree (from a U.S. university or foreign equivalent) plus letters from current or former employers showing five years of experience in the field

FIFTH PREFERENCE EB-5

Another classification of Employment-Based Immigration visa is the EB-5 Immigrant Investor Program. It is designed for entrepreneurs who are investing in commercial enterprise in the United States and who plan to create or preserve at least ten permanent full-time jobs for U.S. citizens.

Exceptional Ability

To be eligible for this EB-2 visa category, individuals must demonstrate that they have exceptional ability in the sciences, arts, or business. This is not the same as having to show extraordinary ability. Individuals who truly have extraordinary ability are few and far between—they are the cream of the crop. But individuals with exceptional ability are more common. Their expertise is significantly beyond that of most workers in their field, but they are not necessarily at the very top of their field.

Proving Exceptional Ability

Individuals in this category must provide at least three of the following types of evidence in order to prove their exceptional ability:

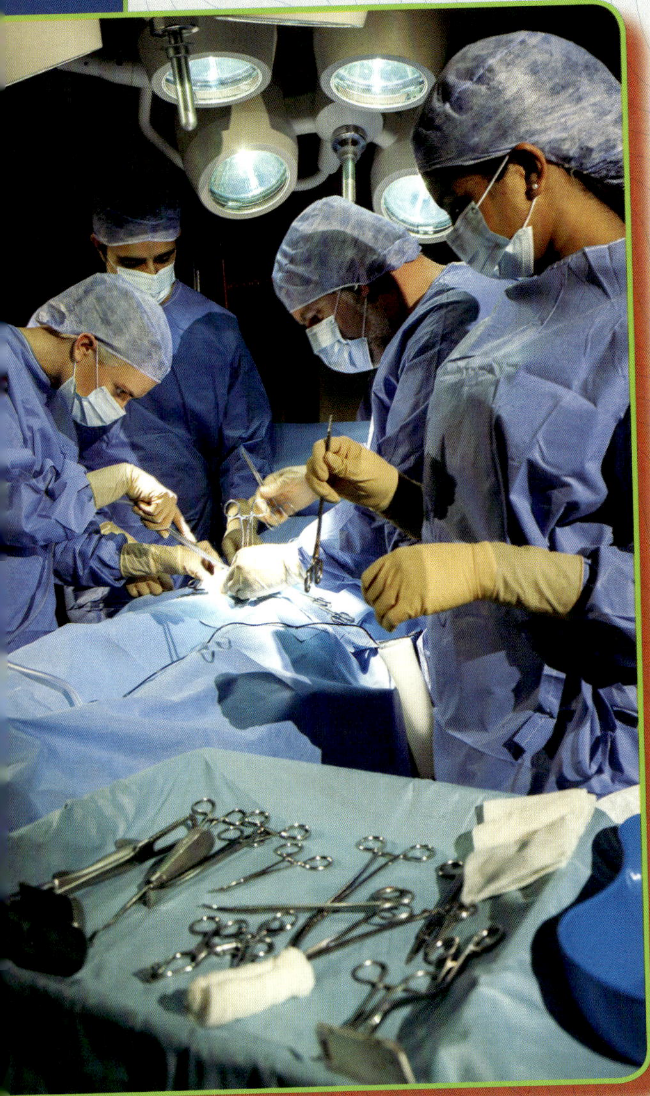

- Official academic record proving the individual has a degree, diploma, or certificate related to the field in which the individual has exceptional ability, from a college, university, or other institution of higher learning
- Letters confirming at least ten years of full-time work in the field
- License or certification to practice the individual's profession or occupation
- A salary that demonstrates the individual's exceptional ability in the field
- Membership in professional associations related to the field
- Recognition for the individual's contributions to the field by peers, government entities, or professional or business organizations
- Other comparable evidence. USCIS doesn't specify what "other comparable evidence" would look like. It would be some other type of tangible proof that the individual has demonstrated exceptional ability in their field.

Professionals with exceptional abilities in a field such as health care may be able to get a national interest waiver.

National Interest Waiver

Most petitions for EB-2 visas must also include Form ETA-750, which is an approved individual labor certification from the Department of Labor. However, that requirement is waived for individuals who are applying for an EB-2 visa under the third category: national interest waiver. These applicants are people whose employment in the United States would greatly benefit the country in some way. The idea behind this visa category is that an applicant's presence in the United States would be in the best interests of the nation.

Most applicants for EB-2 visas must have an employer submit Form I-140, Petition for Alien Worker, to USCIS on their behalf. However, this is not the case for those applying under a national interest waiver—they may file their own labor certification and Form I-140 with USCIS.

Applicants for this category of EB-2 visa must meet at least three of the seven criteria listed above. They must also demonstrate that it is in the United States' best interest that they be allowed to work permanently in the United States.

WHAT ABOUT THE FAMILIES?

Spouses of individuals holding EB-2 visas may be granted entry into the United States under E-21 immigrant status. Children of individuals holding EB-2 visas may be granted entry under E-22 immigrant status, as long as they are under the age of 21.

For many visa categories, the government offers entry to children of immigrants.

The H-1B Visa

While the Employment-Based Immigration visas are all designed for individuals seeking permanent residency, there is another type of employment-based visa designed for temporary residency: the H-1B visa.

Like the O visas, the H-1B visa is considered a nonimmigrant visa. U.S. employers can temporarily employ individuals from foreign countries in specialty occupations by sponsoring them under an H-1B visa. But if the individual ends their employment with the employer, then they must be granted a different nonimmigrant status, find another employer willing to sponsor them under the H-1B visa, or leave the country.

Immigrants having difficulty securing a visa may need to consult with an immigration attorney.

The key to this visa category is that it is for specialty occupations in which jobs require highly specialized knowledge. Jobs that would fall into this category might be in fields such as biotechnology, chemistry, and other physical sciences, or medicine. Other fields could include architecture, engineering, mathematics, accounting, education, law or business specialties, the arts, or theology. One other occupation that can qualify under the H-1B visa category is fashion modeling, as long as the model is considered to be of distinguished merit and ability. In other words, supermodels can apply!

H-1B Limits

H-1B visas are generally good for three years, and they can be extended for up to six years. The United States government has established limits on the number of people who can be offered H-1B status each year. Currently, that limit is 65,000 individuals per year. However, there are certain exemptions from the limit. All individuals holding H-1B visas who work at universities, nonprofit research facilities associated with universities, or government research facilities are exempted from the cap. Also, current laws allow exemptions for up to 20,000 foreign-born individuals who have master's degrees or higher from United States universities.

A Well-Known H-1B Visa Holder

One H-1B visa holder has become extremely well known in the past year: First Lady Melania Trump! The Slovenian fashion model entered the United States in August 1996 on a B-1/B-2 visitor visa, but obtained an H-1B visa in October 1996. Because of Slovenian laws, her H-1B visa was only offered in one-year increments, and she renewed it yearly until 2001, at which point she obtained her green card. She became a United States citizen in 2006, after marrying Donald Trump.

CHAPTER 3 MUSICIANS

People can demonstrate extraordinary ability in a number of different fields, but the arts are an area where numerous famous people over the years have been granted visas based on their talent. Musicians are one such category of artists.

John Lennon was a beloved member of the Beatles. Yoko Ono is a multimedia artist, musician, and peace activist.

THE BALLAD OF JOHN AND YOKO

In March 1969, one of the founding members of the legendary British rock group the Beatles, John Lennon, was on his honeymoon with wife Yoko Ono when he wrote "The Ballad of John and Yoko." The Beatles released the song that same year. It was about the struggles Lennon and Ono faced when they got married.

Although the Beatles and Lennon were widely celebrated superstars, the marriage of John and Yoko was not popular with many of the Beatles' fans. They were a biracial couple in a time of intense racism, and they had begun an affair while John was still married to Cynthia Lennon, the mother of his young son. Some fans felt that Ono was to blame for the eventual breakup of their beloved Beatles.

The song's lyrics seem to predict the upcoming immigration struggles the couple would face. It talks about the couple standing at the dock in Southampton, England, trying to get to Holland or France and being turned away. Later, it speaks of a member of the Beatles' management company arranging for the couple to be able to marry in Gibraltar.

High-Profile Immigrants

Lennon and Ono were both immigrants to the United States. Lennon was born and raised in Liverpool, England, while Ono was born and raised in Tokyo and moved to New York at age 20. The two married in 1969, and the Beatles broke up later that year. Lennon and Ono traveled extensively, and in 1971, they arrived in New York, with Lennon entering on a visitor's visa.

Ono's situation was fairly straightforward, since she had lived in the United States before. However, now she was married to Lennon, and the administration of President Richard Nixon was not happy to have Lennon living in the United States.

At the time, the United States was involved in the Vietnam War, which was incredibly unpopular. Because of the war, Americans were growing increasingly disillusioned and angry with the government. Earlier in the war, the government had glossed over the difficulties going on in Vietnam, but it soon became clear that the reality was very different from the version presented by the government.

The United States' involvement in the Vietnam War left many Americans distrustful of the government. Some of Lennon's songs had a strong antiwar message.

Opposing the War

Gradually, the American public learned that all was not as they had been told in Vietnam. Photojournalism and television news reports made the public aware of what was really going on: the South Vietnamese, along with American military support, were losing the war, and countless lives were being lost in the process.

Antiwar sentiment was high, and John Lennon, a vocal pacifist, added to the protest. Lennon released songs like "Give Peace a Chance" and "Happy Xmas (War Is Over)," both of which were popular among antiwar activists. At the same time, President Nixon was seeking reelection, and he was afraid that Lennon's popular stance might cost him the election. The Nixon administration began deportation proceedings against Lennon and Ono.

Nixon feared that Lennon's message would stir up even more antiwar sentiment, hurting Nixon's chances for reelection.

Arguments for Deportation

Under U.S. law, a person can't be deported simply for exercising freedom of speech, unless they make outright threats to national security. And Lennon hadn't—he simply protested the war and preached peace. However, he had a misdemeanor charge of unlawful cannabis possession in the United Kingdom on his record. The U.S. Immigration and Naturalization Service (which had responsibility for immigration at the time) used this information to argue that he should be considered ineligible for admission to the United States.

Lennon and Ono argued that they needed to remain in the United States because they needed to search for Ono's eight-year-old daughter. Ono's former husband had disappeared with her in the midst of their custody battle. But the government didn't particularly care about Ono's search for her daughter—they simply wanted Lennon and Ono out of the country. The couple hired attorney Leon Wildes, one of the most prominent immigration lawyers in the United States, to help fight their deportation.

Reasons to Stay

Like Lennon, Ono was involved in the arts: she is a multimedia artist, performance artist, singer, songwriter, and moviemaker. Wildes decided to fight the deportation order mainly based on the contributions both Lennon and Ono made to the arts in the United States. Ono was an easy sell. She wasn't as well-known as her husband at that point, so the government agreed to grant her residency in the United States. However, they were less inclined to offer the same residency to the controversial Lennon.

Yoko Ono didn't have nearly as much difficulty gaining residency as John Lennon did.

POWERFUL SUPPORTERS

Lennon and Ono had influential friends who spoke out in support. They were joined by thousands of ordinary young people, who launched a campaign that was often called "Let Them Stay in the USA." The musician Bob Dylan even wrote a letter to INS on Lennon and Ono's behalf. The letter argued that Lennon and Ono's art was a breath of fresh air when compared to more commercial, manufactured music.

Dylan's letter was only one of hundreds that were sent to the government in support of the couple. Ultimately, though, the campaign didn't particularly help Lennon's cause. Nixon was determined to deport him—but then Nixon's involvement in the Watergate scandal came to light, leaving the president with much bigger problems on his hands. As a result of the scandal he resigned from the presidency, and his successor, Gerald Ford, did not pursue the deportation of Lennon. The deportation order was overturned in 1975. It was a long, nearly four-year battle, but it finally came to an end, with Lennon being granted a green card in 1976.

Musicians Joan Baez and Bob Dylan both supported Lennon's desire to stay in the United States.

Bieber Fever

Another musician has been granted a visa based on extraordinary ability, but much more recently: the Canadian Justin Bieber. Bieber's career began when he was discovered through covers of songs he had performed on YouTube videos. His immigration story is less drama-filled than Lennon's, but it has some bumps in the road, too. He is currently in the United States on an O-1 nonimmigrant visa, but he may have originally entered the country on a visitor visa, given that he arrived in the United States before he had recorded his first album and become an international star.

Canadian Justin Bieber lives in the United States but hasn't expressed any interest in becoming a citizen.

O-1 OR VISITOR VISA?

Someone like Bieber, who came to the United States to meet with a music industry professional, would likely first enter the country on a visitor visa. However, it's also possible that he entered on an O-1 visa, gained on the basis of his millions of YouTube views. Similarly, British singer Adele would likely be able to easily secure an O-1 visa, given her phenomenal success in the music industry. Her immigration status is unknown, but she does own a home in California, so presumably she intends to spend a fair amount of time in the United States.

Rising Star

Bieber's career quickly took off, and he soon became a huge star. In theory, he could probably apply for permanent residency based on his extraordinary ability as a musician. But Bieber reportedly has no desire to do so. He remains strongly loyal to Canada. In a 2011 interview with *Rolling Stone*, he joked when asked about becoming a U.S. citizen. "You guys are evil," he said. "Canada's the best country in the world. We go to the doctor and we don't need to worry about paying him, but here, your whole life, you're broke because of medical bills. My bodyguard's baby was premature, and now he has to pay for it. In Canada, if your baby's premature, he stays in the hospital as long as he needs to, and then you go home."

Another Famous YouTuber

PERSONAL STORIES

Justin Bieber isn't the only artist to claim "extraordinary ability" on the basis of YouTube views. South Korean–born singer, songwriter, and rapper Park Jae-sang, more commonly known as Psy, became internationally known in 2012, when his music video for "Gangnam Style" became the first YouTube video to hit one billion views. As of late 2016, the video has had more than 2.7 billion views! Bieber and Psy actually share the same talent manager, Scooter Braun. Like Bieber, Psy holds an O-1 visa based on his extraordinary ability in music.

Calls for Deportation

Bieber may have no interest in becoming an American citizen, but he still needs permission to continue living here. Technically, the U.S. government could potentially deport Bieber, although they're not very likely to do so. Bieber has had several run-ins with the law in recent years, including a Florida arrest for DUI, driving with an expired license, and resisting arrest.

After his DUI arrest, hundreds of thousands of people petitioned for Bieber's deportation, but the government did not take any action. DUI is not typically considered a deportable offense, although the circumstances surrounding the DUI may make it one. Still, trying to deport Bieber could easily turn into a long legal battle, and the Obama administration didn't appear inclined to pursue deportation for the musician. It is a very different situation from the Nixon administration's stance with John Lennon!

CHAPTER 4

ATHLETES

David Beckham played soccer for the LA Galaxy from 2007 to 2012.

Another category of individuals who may be granted a visa on the basis of extraordinary ability are athletes. If an athlete performs at the very top of their sport, they can apply for a visa based on their athletic ability.

The Amazing David Beckham

Soccer is an incredibly popular sport worldwide—in fact, many sources claim that it is by far the most popular sport in terms of fans. However, it hasn't gained nearly the same popularity in the United States, which is more focused on football, baseball, basketball, and hockey.

International Star

The popularity of soccer in the United States got a boost when star player David Beckham arrived to play for a Major League Soccer team. In 2007, Beckham accepted a deal to play for the LA Galaxy under a five-year, $32.5-million contract. It was an incredibly high-profile deal, as Beckham was, at the time, one of the most famous soccer players in the world. Lucrative endorsement deals meant that Beckham stood to earn far more than the $32.5 million covered by his contract, and Major League Soccer stood to gain major visibility in the sports world.

Gaining a Visa

Beckham's stellar career playing for Manchester United and the Spanish team Real Madrid, as well as for England's national team, had made him a worldwide star. He was easily eligible for an O-1 visa, based on his extraordinary athletic ability. He and his wife, Victoria, own a home in California, though they are not United States citizens. Both still hold British citizenship, with no apparent plans to change that.

POSH'S VISA

PERSONAL STORIES

Victoria Beckham became famous as a member of the all-women pop group Spice Girls, where she was known as Posh Spice. In addition to being a singing star, she's also been a model and is a well-known fashion designer and businesswoman. So while she could have entered the United States on an O-3 visa as the wife of David Beckham, she also could have entered with her own O-1 visa, as she has demonstrated extraordinary ability in her own fields. Visas are generally confidential unless the person chooses to disclose them, so while David Beckham is known to have an O-1 visa, Victoria's type of visa is unknown.

Victoria Beckham has built a successful career as an entrepreneur.

A Star from an Earlier Generation

Long before David Beckham arrived in the United States, another world-famous soccer star had also entered on an O-1 visa. Pelé, whose given name is Edson Arantes Do Nascimento, was an internationally known soccer star before soccer was even really played at a professional level in the United States. (Soccer was played in the United States as early as the 1850s, but then it had declined by the 1930s. It did not regain any real popularity in the country until the 1960s.)

Pelé was one of the stars of Brazil's national soccer team, and he made his mark at the 1958, 1962, 1966, and 1970 World Cups. Brazil won three of those tournaments, making Pelé—his country's all-time top goalscorer in men's soccer—the only player to have won three times. He remains the most successful men's soccer player in the world in terms of goals scored, with a reported 1,281 goals scored in 1,363 games.

In 1975, Pelé moved to the United States to play for the New York Cosmos, making him the first well-known player in U.S. professional soccer. His agreement to play for the Cosmos brought significant attention to soccer in the United States. Pelé played for the team until 1977, when he retired from the sport.

For many decades, Pelé has been one of the most famous faces in the world of international soccer.

Returning to the United States

After his retirement, Pelé returned to Brazil for many years, but in 2011 he sought to return to the United States to start work as Honorary President of the New York Cosmos. It reportedly took seven months for Pelé's immigration attorney, Michael Wildes, to secure an O-1 visa based on Pelé's extraordinary ability as an athlete. According to some sources, it only took two weeks for David Beckham to secure the same visa.

A FAMILY BUSINESS

Michael Wildes of the law firm Wildes & Weinberg helped Pelé secure his O-1 visa. This certainly wasn't the firm's first high-profile case, though. Wildes' father, Leon Wildes, is the immigration attorney who fought John Lennon and Yoko Ono's deportation case in the early 1970s. The firm has also represented celebrities including racing driver Dario Franchitti, basketball star Kwame James, singers Joe Cocker and Johnny Rotten, supermodel Gisele Bündchen, and classical singer Sarah Brightman.

Singer Joe Cocker retained the services of Wildes & Weinberg in his own immigration battle.

Basketball Star Dirk Nowitzki

Athletes with extraordinary ability aren't limited to soccer players. Dirk Nowitzki, the seven-foot-tall (2.1-m) power forward for the Dallas Mavericks, is proof of that! Many commentators consider Nowitzki to be one of the top power forwards in basketball history.

Nowitzki is the highest-scoring foreign player in NBA history, with nearly 30,000 regular-season points to his credit, and he was named the NBA's Most Valuable Player in 2007. Nowitzki comes from an incredibly athletic family. His mother was a professional basketball player in Germany in the 1960s, and his father was a high-ranked handball player. His older sister was a track and field champion and also played basketball.

Attracting Attention

Nowitzki enjoyed a successful basketball career for several years in Germany, but he began to gain attention in the United States when, at age 19, he participated in the Nike Hoop Heroes Tour and played against NBA stars. He played better than NBA legend Charles Barkley, and Barkley reportedly called him a genius and offered him help in finding a contract in the NBA. The next year, Nowitzki participated in the Nike Hoop Summit and caught the attention of numerous scouts from the NBA and European basketball clubs.

Dirk Nowitski has had a stellar career playing for the Dallas Mavericks.

Nowitzki set his sights on the NBA and was drafted by the Dallas Mavericks in 1998. His NBA career got off to a slow start, as the 20-year-old basketball player struggled with his confidence and with a lockout on the basketball season due to salary disputes. But in the seasons that followed, Nowitzki steadily improved, and is now one of the NBA's top players.

Nowitzki is still a German citizen and plays under an extraordinary ability visa based on his athletic skill. However, in 2012 he told journalists that he might consider applying for United States citizenship in the future.

Nowitzki received an ESPY Award for Best Male Athlete in 2011.

IMMIGRATION AND THE NBA

Dirk Nowitzki is not the only immigrant playing in the NBA. President Donald Trump's attempted ban on immigration from seven predominantly Muslim countries posed possible problems for the NBA. Two of the league's players—Luol Deng of the Lakers and Bucks player Thon Maker—are Sudanese, and Sudan is on the list of countries from which Trump wants to ban immigrants from entering the United States. Their future as basketball players in the United States may be affected by immigration policy.

Two Countries

Applying for U.S. citizenship doesn't necessarily mean that he would give up his German citizenship. Nowitzki has said that he is proud of his German background and would like to live in both Germany and the United States when he retires from basketball. He even carried the German flag at the opening ceremony of the 2008 Olympic Games in Beijing, despite having spent the last decade in the United States. Perhaps dual citizenship will ultimately be in his future.

Although he plays professional basketball in the United States, Nowitzki represented Germany at the 2008 Olympics in Beijing.

DUAL CITIZENSHIP

Dual citizenship was actually banned in the United States for many years, but in 1967 the Supreme Court struck down many of the laws that forbid it. When immigrants take the Oath of Allegiance to become a U.S. citizen, they may have to give up their original citizenship as well, depending on the laws of their home country. If a U.S. citizen becomes a citizen of another country that does not require immigrants to renounce their former citizenship, that person can end up with dual citizenship. A number of well-known actors and actresses enjoy dual citizenship, including Jim Carrey (Canada), Nicole Kidman (Australia), Natalie Portman (Israel), Olivia Wilde (Ireland), Angelina Jolie (Cambodia), Kirsten Dunst (Germany), Salma Hayek (Mexico), and Charlize Theron (South Africa).

Nowitzki's wife, Jessica Olsson, is not an American citizen, either. She is a Kenyan-born Swedish national. However, the couple's two children were both born in the United States, making them U.S. citizens.

When Ability Isn't Quite Extraordinary

For most major international superstars, such as David Beckham and Dirk Nowitzki, getting a visa based on extraordinary athletic ability isn't too difficult. For some, like Pelé, it takes time—but it's doable. But what if a person is less well known, but still an accomplished athlete?

Afshin Noroozi, an Iranian table tennis player, found out in 2012. Noroozi was the first Iranian table tennis player ever to compete in the Olympics, and in 2010 he sought a United States visa on the basis of extraordinary athletic ability. His application was based on the fact that he finished 65th at the 2008 Olympics and was ranked the 284th best table tennis player in the world.

Athletes applying for visas can possess extraordinary ability in any sport—even table tennis.

Visa Withdrawn

USCIS initially granted Noroozi's visa, but then revoked it in 2011, based on new immigration rulings. Noroozi filed another visa petition, but USCIS denied it. They did not agree that his athletic ability fell in the realm of "extraordinary ability." Their ruling stated that he did not adequately show that he played a leading role in the success of Iranian table tennis. His successes were not reported by major publications, and he did not adequately demonstrate how his presence in the United States would benefit the country.

Appealing the Decision

Noroozi worked with immigration attorney John Assadi to appeal the decision. He eventually filed a lawsuit against Homeland Security Secretary Janet Napolitano and Attorney General Eric Holder, on the basis of racial discrimination. However, Manhattan Federal District Court judge Paul Engelmayer upheld USCIS's decision. His view was that a ranking of 284th in the world did not mean that Noroozi made up part of the "small percentage who have risen to the very top of the field of endeavor," which is who extraordinary ability visas were created for.

If USCIS had granted Noroozi's request for an extraordinary ability visa on the basis of his table tennis performance, they would theoretically have then had to grant similar visas for the top 284 players in every other sport as well. This could potentially lead to a major influx of athletes who may want to enter or become citizens of the United States.

Noroozi was ready to take his case to the Supreme Court if necessary, but it ended at the district court level.

TEMPORARY U.S. ENTRY

Foreign athletes coming into the United States have another option if they are coming solely for the purpose of competing in a specific event. The P-1A Internationally Recognized Athlete visa allows accomplished foreign athletes to come into the United States to compete, either as individuals or as part of a team. The P-1A visa allows individual athletes to stay as long as they need to complete the event, up to five years. They can also get a single extension of up to five more years if needed to complete the event, but the total stay cannot exceed ten years. If the athlete is part of a team, the P-1A visa allows a stay of up to one year to complete the event. Extensions can be granted in one-year increments if needed to complete the event.

CHAPTER 5 MEDIA PERSONALITIES

Musicians and athletes aren't the only notable celebrities who can be granted a visa on the basis of extraordinary ability. Political and media personalities can also enter the United States under this visa, provided they can prove they meet the eligibility requirements.

A Controversial Figure

Piers Morgan is a British citizen who currently lives and works in New York. He is editor-at-large of the U.S.-based operation of the Mail Online news website. He is also living proof that the immigration process can be very difficult, even if you are a celebrity.

Before coming to the United States, Morgan was well known in England as a writer for several tabloids. He shot to fame when he was named editor of the tabloid *News of the World* in 1994, becoming the youngest editor of a national British newspaper in more than 50 years. He later expanded into television, appearing on shows such as *Britain's Got Talent*, *Good Morning Britain*, and numerous other shows.

Piers Morgan has been a familiar face for many years due to his frequent appearances on television.

Although he was popular on *Britain's Got Talent*, Morgan was not always well liked as the host of *Piers Morgan Live*.

Moving to the United States

In 2010, Morgan was offered a job in the United States. *Larry King Live* had run on CNN for 25 years, and upon King's retirement the network planned to replace his show with *Piers Morgan Live*. But there was a problem—Morgan ran into difficulty getting the appropriate visa from USCIS.

Morgan already had a visa that allowed him to work part-time as a judge on the television show *America's Got Talent*. However, he needed a different type of work visa to allow him to work on *Piers Morgan Live*, which would be a full-time assignment. Unfortunately, he applied for the new visa during a time when the government was tightening down on immigration and the process was significantly slowed down. This left Morgan in limbo, wondering whether he would be able to accept the position offered by CNN.

THE BRITISH REACTION

PERSONAL STORIES

Morgan's visa difficulties became a source of amusement, particularly among British journalists. Morgan was (and still is) a controversial, polarizing figure, and he had made many enemies during his career in journalism. The details of visa applications and decisions are confidential, but there was much speculation that the reason for the delay may have been due to his unpopularity.

Speculation Mounts

Morgan was well known as a media personality, so he almost certainly could have gained access to the United States with an O-1 visa. In the absence of verifiable facts, journalists speculated that perhaps Morgan did not want to enter under an O-1 visa, which would have made him a nonimmigrant. They wondered if Morgan was pushing for a chance at permanent U.S. residency. Whatever the truth of the delay is, it's confidential. News service Reuters reported that Morgan ultimately took the position with CNN after securing an O-1 nonimmigrant visa.

Even though his immigration status is now secure, he hasn't made himself any more popular since arriving! *Piers Morgan Live* ran until 2014, and after that Morgan took the editor-at-large position at Mail Online. His story certainly serves as proof that you don't necessarily have to be a well-liked personality to obtain a visa based on extraordinary ability—just a sufficiently famous one who meets the eligibility criteria.

The Mail Online website, which Morgan heads up, is one of the most popular news websites in the United Kingdom.

Speaking Out

During his years in the United States, Morgan's opinions and his willingness to speak bluntly have made him more than a few enemies. After the 2012 shooting of 20 elementary school students and six adult staff members at Sandy Hook Elementary School in Newtown, Connecticut, Morgan spoke forcefully about the need for stronger gun-control laws in the United States. His words angered those Americans who fiercely believe in the Second Amendment right to bear arms.

More than 100,000 Americans signed a petition to deport Morgan based on his statements, but the White House declined to pursue it. They felt that Morgan's First Amendment rights protected his right to free speech. Morgan replied to the controversy by writing in the *Daily Mail*:

> I can spare those Americans who want me deported a lot of effort by saying this: If you don't change your gun laws to at least try to stop this relentless tidal wave of murderous carnage, then you don't have to worry about deporting me. Although I love the country as a second home and one that has treated me incredibly well, I would, as a concerned parent first—and latterly, of a one-year-old daughter who may attend an American elementary school like Sandy Hook in three years' time—seriously consider deporting myself.

Morgan made a lot of enemies when he waded into the gun control debate.

Clive Crook

Piers Morgan is one of the best known current media personalities living in the United States under an O-1 visa, but there are others as well. One less polarizing media personality is Clive Crook, who is a columnist, commentator, and editor on topics of economics, finance, and politics.

Crook was born in Yorkshire, England, and was educated in the United Kingdom as well. He came to the United States to work in the media and has worked for several notable publications, including *The Atlantic* and *The Economist*. Currently, he works for Bloomberg News.

All media personalities have both fans and people who disagree with them, and Crook is no exception. However, he isn't nearly as polarizing a public figure as Piers Morgan. Crook and Morgan tend to be on opposite ends of the political spectrum in some ways—while Morgan generally supports Republican President Donald Trump, Crook has made no secret of the fact that he finds the Trump administration to be quite incompetent.

Clive Crook had a successful career in the United Kingdom before moving to the United States.

WHAT'S IN A NAME?

GENIUS VISAS

The term "genius visa" typically refers to the O-1 and EB-1 visas for extraordinary ability. It's a short, catchy way to encapsulate the fact that the people getting these visas tend to be geniuses in their particular field.

Are Genius Visas Fair?

In January 2014, Crook wrote a column for Bloomberg View, entitled "I Was a Genius Just Like Justin Bieber." In it, Crook talks about the "genius visa" that Bieber has, and how to get one.

"I used to have an O-1 myself, and was very pleased about it until I realized that, legally speaking, genius simply means 'has the resources to navigate an insanely complex application process,'" Crook wrote.

While individuals do need to have extraordinary ability to qualify for a genius visa, they also need to have the resources to complete the incredibly complicated application process. Immigration lawyers can help their clients navigate the process, but their fees are often high.

Media personalities like Clive Crook generally have the resources to get the help they need, but that's not the case for everyone. It's just one of many sticky situations in U.S. immigration—the question of whether policy is fair for both the extraordinary and the ordinary.

Genius visas aren't necessarily for geniuses—just for people who have extraordinary ability in their field.

CHAPTER 6

SCIENTISTS AND ENTREPRENEURS

It's easy to see how major celebrities such as John Lennon, Justin Bieber, and David Beckham qualify for genius visas and enter the United States. However, some "geniuses" have a lower profile. These often include academics, researchers, scientists, and entrepreneurs. They may be at the very top of their field, but their field is much less visible than sports, movies, or television.

BY THE NUMBERS

The numbers of O-1 visas issued each year were discussed in Chapter 1, but what about EB-1 and HB-1 visas? The government has a cap on each, which is calculated using complex formulas. In general, the government issues around 40,000 EB-1 visas each year. The number of H-1B visas issued each year is capped at around 85,000.

Boy Genius and Entrepreneur: Josh Buckley

Josh Buckley is just one of many young tech entrepreneurs to find their fortune in San Francisco.

UK-born Josh Buckley is the founder and CEO of Mino Games, a San Francisco–based video game development company that has released the popular Mino Monsters mobile games. Buckley built his first video game at age 12 and sold his first company at age 15 for a sum in the low six figures. It seems fair to say that Buckley had demonstrated exceptional ability in the field of computer programming.

Before he was 20, Buckley decided to move to the United States to further his career development. Normally, a tech genius like Buckley might apply for an H-1B visa, since he works in a specialized field. However, the H-1B generally isn't an option for people who are self-employed, as Buckley was. Also, the H-1B requires a college degree, which Buckley did not have.

Instead, Buckley opted for an O-1 visa, which doesn't require a college degree. However, the young Irishman John Collison, a fellow entrepreneur and a Harvard University dropout, found during his application process that USCIS expects to see a degree—and that the process is somewhat more difficult for those who don't have one. Buckley ran into the same problem. To support his visa request, he had to get letters of support from Apple co-founder Steve Wozniak and Netscape co-founder Marc Andreessen. Both Buckley and Collison eventually obtained their O-1 visas.

SERGEY BRIN

PERSONAL STORIES

In 1980, a six-year-old boy left the Soviet Union with his parents. They were a Jewish family fleeing religious persecution. His parents were educated people who were reduced to working at lower-level jobs. They came to the United States to improve their son's chances for a productive life. Their difficult move paid off—16 years later, their son, Sergey Brin, co-founded the tech giant Google. Google is now everywhere, and Brin has a net worth of more than $39 billion.

Google now employs many immigrants and U.S. citizens.

Excellence Nearly Denied

A few years ago, a doctor from India was working as an assistant professor in Nebraska under an EB-1 visa. His specialization was in the field of cardiovascular medicine and public health. The doctor was sent a Request for Evidence by USCIS, which can sometimes be a first step toward a visa petition being denied.

Worried that he might be deported, the doctor contacted an immigration law firm to help him prepare the material needed to support his petition. The doctor hadn't yet gained national or international acclaim, so he needed to prove how crucial his work in his field was to U.S. public health.

His immigration attorneys focused on the significance of his published work in the field. They also researched similar cases where individuals had been granted a visa based on lesser accomplishments in similar fields. Within three months, the doctor's petition for a visa was approved. It turned out to be a decision that would benefit the United States. The doctor made a significant impact when the U.S. Food and Drug Administration issued a warning for the antidepressant Celexa, based on his research.

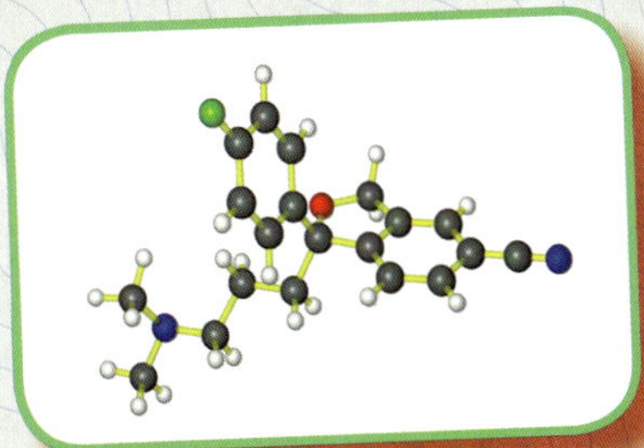

This is a molecular model of Celexa, a widely prescribed antidepressant.

What About the Jobs?

Some people worry that genius visas result in jobs being taken away from American citizens. But some employers feel they can't find the talented individuals they need in the United States. There is a large pool of foreign talent, especially in STEM careers, to choose from. While there is a movement in the United States to put more resources into STEM training, it hasn't yet come as far as it has in some other countries.

Helping the Country?

Many people argue that talented foreign workers can actually bring more jobs to the United States. For example, they may start companies that can then employ Americans. Google, which was co-founded by the immigrant Sergey Brin, now employs more than 57,000 people. Employing immigrants does not come at the cost of rejecting U.S. citizens. Microsoft co-founder Bill Gates has said that for every one immigrant Microsoft hires, they hire four U.S. citizens.

Kim Berry, a spokesman for the Programmers Guild, is in favor of suspending the H-1B visa program. However, he supports the O-1 program, because it brings in extremely talented individuals. Speaking on behalf of the Programmers Guild, he said that the O-1 visa helped the United States by bringing in the brightest and the best entrepreneurs.

Changes to Immigration Policy

President Trump has spoken often about the H-1B program—and his opinions on it have gone back and forth. While on the campaign trail in 2016, his original statements about the program were harsh. But in a campaign debate he said, "I'm softening the position...because we have to have talented people in this country." Later, he issued a press release saying, "I will end forever the use of the H-1B as a cheap labor program, and institute an absolute requirement to hire American workers first for every visa and immigration program. No exceptions." He seemed to reinforce this in his inauguration speech in January 2017, where he claimed, "We will follow two simple rules: buy American and hire American."

President Trump's views on the H-1B visa program may affect future policy.

THE FUTURE FOR IMMIGRANTS OF EXTRAORDINARY ABILITY

The face of immigration in the United States is changing rapidly under the Trump administration. Within his first two weeks in office, President Trump attempted to make sweeping changes to immigration, including banning immigrants from seven predominantly Muslim countries: Syria, Iraq, Iran, Sudan, Somalia, Yemen, and Libya. This ban would affect immigrants in all categories, including O-1, EB, and H-1B visas.

Due to what many people see as religious discrimination, his executive order has been challenged in the courts. A second proposed version left Iran off the list of banned countries. It's worth noting that these countries have produced many well-known and influential executives in the United States. For example, there are high-profile executives of Iranian descent at tech giants Yahoo, Google, Twitter, and eBay. And Steve Jobs, the well-known genius and co-founder behind Apple Computer, was of Syrian descent.

Syrian-descended Steve Jobs created thousands of jobs when he built Apple into a worldwide brand.

An Uncertain Future

After Trump ordered the ban, one immigration attorney began telling her immigrant clients not to leave the United States, because she couldn't guarantee they'd be let back in. She also advised those abroad to come back as soon as possible, and to be prepared to face questioning and possible refusal. Universities around the United States began issuing similar warnings to their students and academics: we want you here and value your contribution, but we can't guarantee you'll be let back in if you leave—so don't leave.

Immigrants can still leave the United States, but for some, it's questionable whether they'll be allowed back in.

FURTHER IMPACT OF THE MUSLIM BAN

One concern about Trump's proposed ban is that it will incite international disapproval that could impact major international events. For example, Los Angeles is bidding to host the 2024 Olympics, and the United States wishes to host the World Cup in 2026. If international officials associated with events like these disagree with Trump's proposed ban, it could ruin the United States' chances of being chosen to host those events and other similar ones.

Worrying About the Future

Many individuals currently living and working in the United States under genius visas are understandably concerned. Jordanian citizen Zafer Younis is a partner at a venture capital firm that invests heavily in startup companies in predominantly Muslim countries. Although Jordan is not on President Trump's list of banned countries, it is a predominantly Muslim country, so Younis worries that it will eventually be added. "My wife is here. I have upcoming business trips to Japan and Europe. I'm not affected, yet I have to think twice—do I really need to travel or not? It's a feeling I thought I left back in the Middle East. It's an anxiety, that things are beyond your control," he said in a 2017 interview.

Younis has a valid concern, and only time will tell how the changes to immigration policy will ultimately affect the businesses that have, for the past several decades, hired foreign talent. Will foreign workers still be willing to come to the United States to work, knowing that their future may be insecure? And will businesses be willing to hire foreign workers, knowing that same instability exists?

One thing is certain: the face of the tech, academic, and research fields in the United States could change significantly if immigrants of extraordinary ability are no longer able to enter the United States.

GLOSSARY

academic Someone or something involved with higher education, or another community that is concerned with research, education, and scholarship.
affiliate An organization that is somehow connected to another, usually larger, organization.
biracial Involving members of two races.
CEO Chief executive officer, the highest-ranking person in a company.
consulate The office where a government consul carries out his or her duties in a foreign country.
consultation The process of discussing something. In immigration, it means a written statement by an applicant's peers testifying to the applicant's ability in their field.
DUI The offense of driving under the influence of drugs or alcohol.
embassy The residence of an ambassador.
evidentiary Providing evidence.
indentured servant An immigrant who was bound by contract to work for a specified period of time to pay off his or her passage to North America.
multinational Involving more than one nation.
pacifist A person who believes war is unjustifiable.
Panama Canal Zone A former U.S. territory in Panama that included the Panama Canal and the immediate area on either side. The territory was dissolved in 1979.
petitioner A person who is requesting a visa for a potential employee of foreign descent.
photojournalism The communication of news through photographs.
refugees People who have been forced to flee their country to avoid persecution, political danger, or natural disaster.
Soviet Union A former federation of countries under communist rule, including Russia and numerous Eastern European and Baltic countries. The Soviet Union was dissolved in 1991.
STEM Shorthand term referring to the study of science, technology, engineering, and mathematics.
subsidiary A company controlled by a parent company.
tabloid A popular, usually sensationalistic, newspaper.
tenure Guaranteed permanent employment in the field of academia.
theology The study of religion and the nature of God.
venture capital A firm that invests in new, potentially risky, startup businesses.
Watergate scandal A political scandal in the 1970s that ultimately brought about President Nixon's resignation.
World Cup An international soccer tournament that takes place every four years.

FOR MORE INFORMATION

BOOKS

Buckley, James. *Pelé*. New York: DK Biography, 2007.

Geoffreys, Clayton. *Dirk Nowitzki: The Inspiring Story of One of Basketball's Best European Stars*. Winter Park, FL: Calvintir Books, 2016.

Housel, Debra J. *Famous Immigrants: The 20th Century*. Huntington Beach, CA: Teacher Created Materials, 2007.

Howell, Sara. *Famous Immigrants and Their Stories*. New York: Rosen Publishing Group, 2014.

WEBSITES

Find out more about immigration at the U.S. Citizenship and Immigration Services:
www.uscis.gov

Discover more at the Made Into America: Immigrant Stories Archive:
www.madeintoamerica.org

INDEX